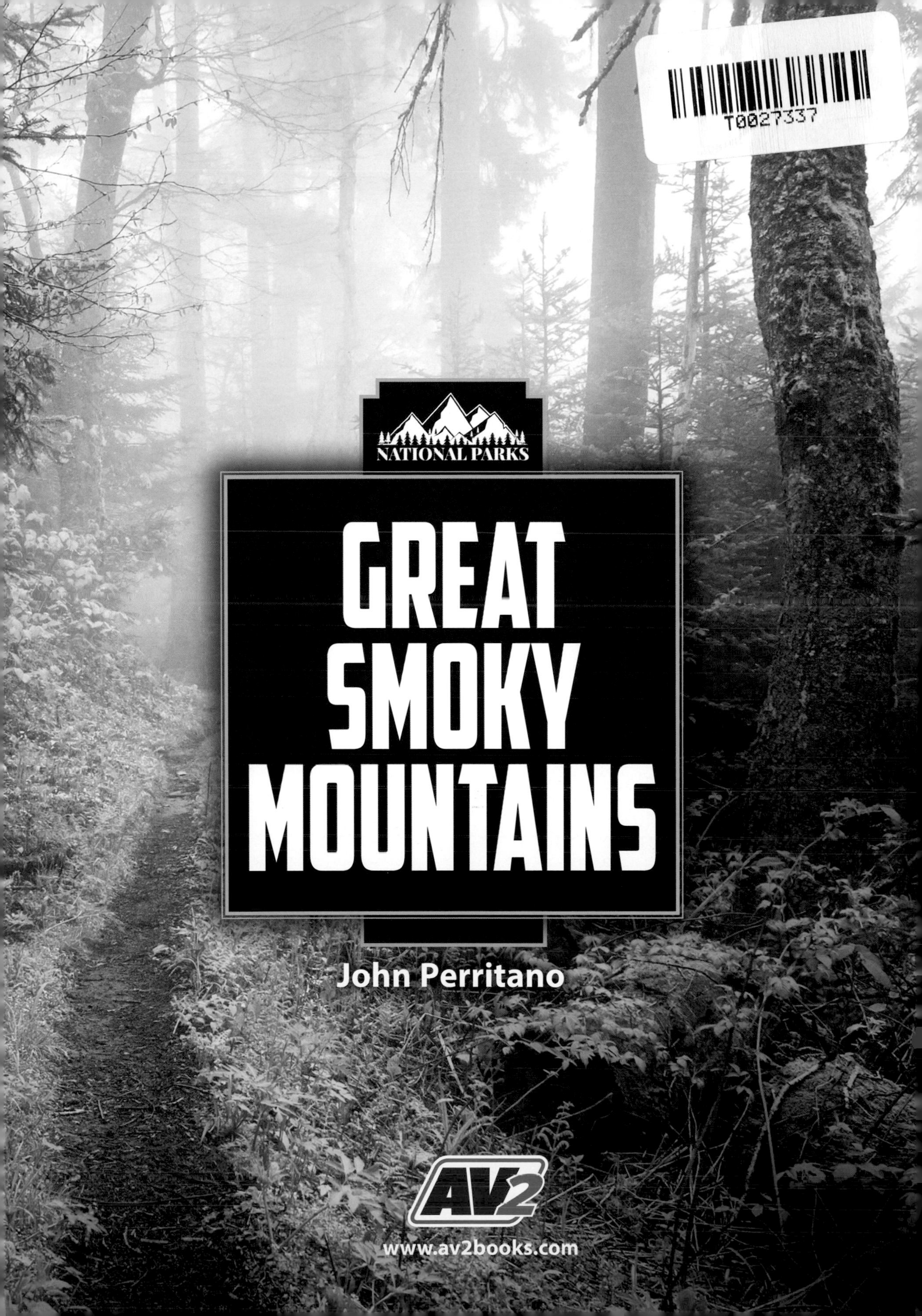
T0027337
NATIONAL PARKS
GREAT
SMOKY
MOUNTAINS
John Perritano
AV2
www.av2books.com

Step 1
Go to **www.av2books.com**

Step 2
Enter this unique code
MHUTFZSV8

Step 3
Explore your interactive eBook!

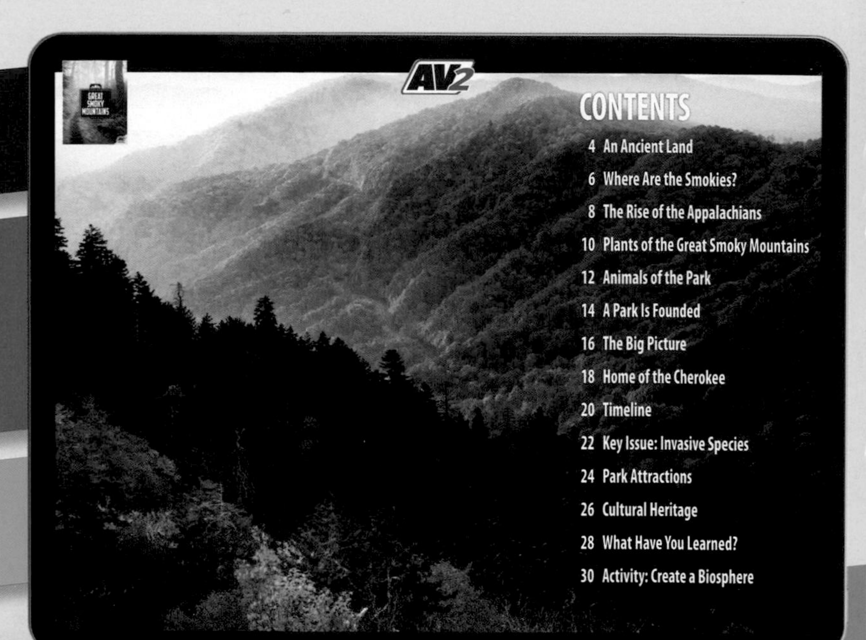

AV2 is optimized for use on any device

Your interactive eBook comes with...

Contents
Browse a live contents page to easily navigate through resources

Audio
Listen to sections of the book read aloud

Videos
Watch informative video clips

Weblinks
Gain additional information for research

Try This!
Complete activities and hands-on experiments

Key Words
Study vocabulary, and complete a matching word activity

Quizzes
Test your knowledge

Slideshows
View images and captions

... and much, much more!

NATIONAL PARKS

GREAT SMOKY MOUNTAINS

CONTENTS

An Ancient Land

The forests of Great Smoky Mountains National Park radiate with vibrant greens, golds, and reds. Rounded mountaintops are often shrouded in morning fog. Located along the border of Tennessee and North Carolina, the Great Smoky Mountains, or "Smokies," are ancient. They have been part of North America for hundreds of millions of years.

The Smokies have rich, fertile soil that produces a variety of plants. Their woodlands and valleys are home to many animal **species**. There is more to this land than nature, however. The Smokies are the **ancestral** home of the Cherokee. Both the Cherokee and their land experienced dramatic changes when European settlers arrived.

Great Smoky Mountains National Park covers an area of **522,427 acres** (211,419 hectares).

At **6,643 feet** (2,025 meters), Clingmans Dome is the park's **highest peak**. It also the highest peak in Tennessee.

Clingmans Dome

The park has about **2,100 miles** (3,380 kilometers) of streams running through it.

The Great Smoky Mountains get their name from the natural fog that sometimes covers their peaks.

In time, the U.S. government realized the importance of preserving the Great Smoky Mountains and made the area a national park. Today, it is the most visited national park in the United States. More than 11 million people come here every year to take in the sights.

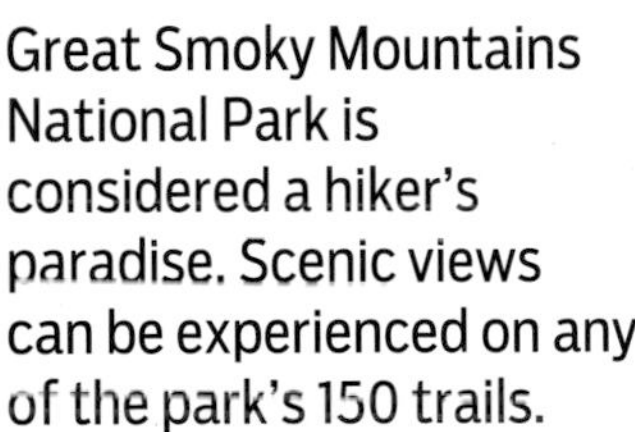

Great Smoky Mountains National Park is considered a hiker's paradise. Scenic views can be experienced on any of the park's 150 trails.

MAPPING GREAT SMOKY MOUNTAINS

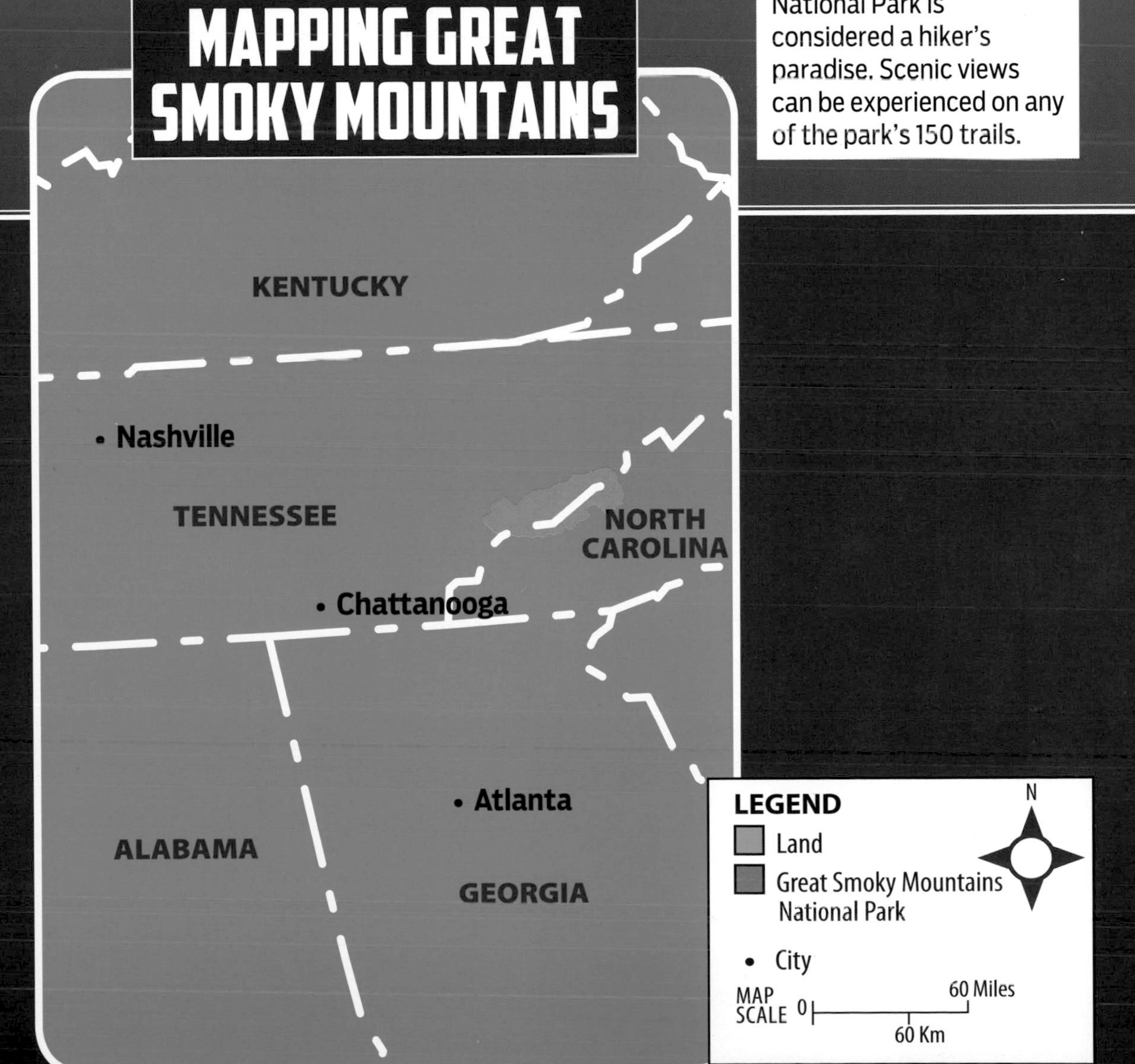

Where Are the Smokies?

Located southeast of Knoxville, Tennessee, the Great Smoky Mountains are part of the Appalachian Mountains. This is a series of mountain ranges that extend all the way from Canada to Alabama. The Smokies are found in the southern part of the larger mountain system. The highest mountains within the Smokies are contained within the national park.

People coming to the park can do so through three main entrances and several smaller ones. Oconaluftee is the main entrance on the North Carolina side. It is found in the town of Cherokee. The other main entrances, Sugarlands and Cades Cove, are located in Tennessee. Sugarlands is just outside the town of Gatlinburg. Cades Cove is a few miles (km) south of Townsend.

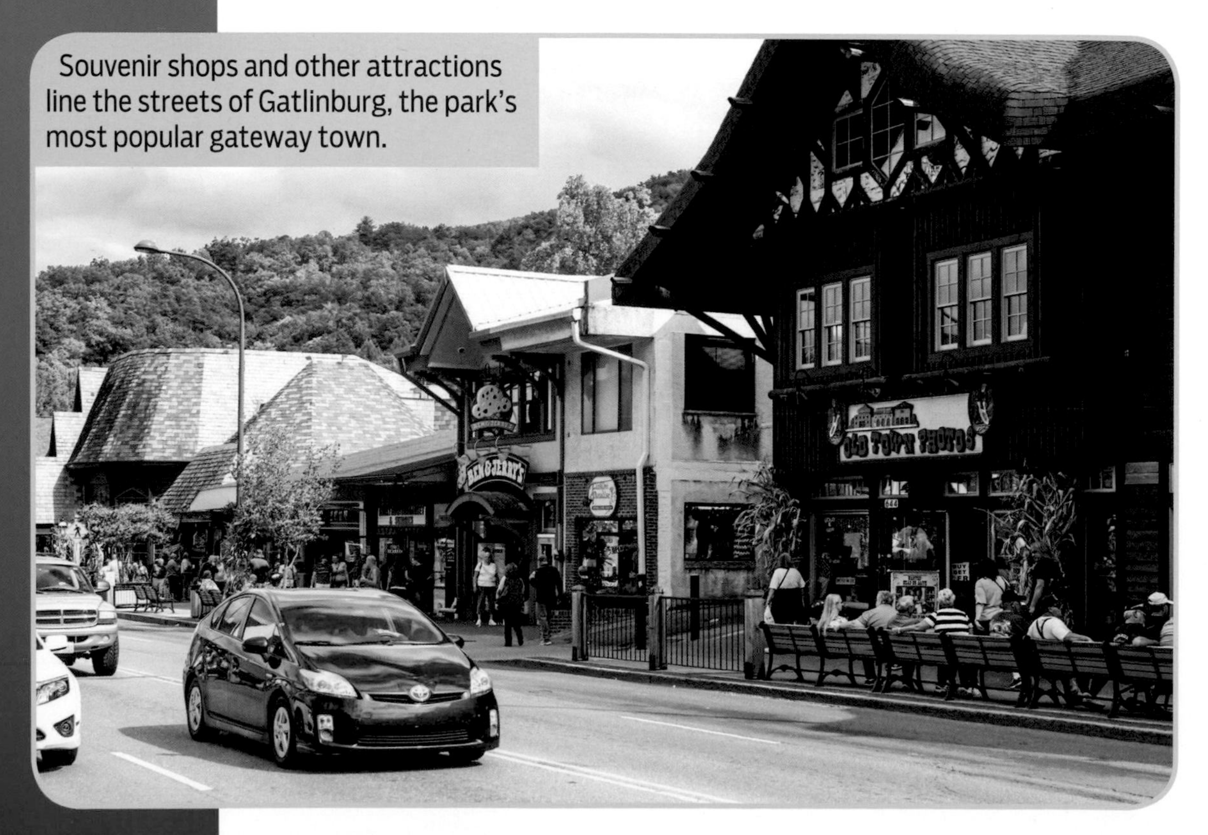

Souvenir shops and other attractions line the streets of Gatlinburg, the park's most popular gateway town.

PUZZLER

The Appalachians are made up of approximately 70 smaller mountain ranges.

Q: Can you identify each of these smaller mountain ranges within the Appalachian Range?

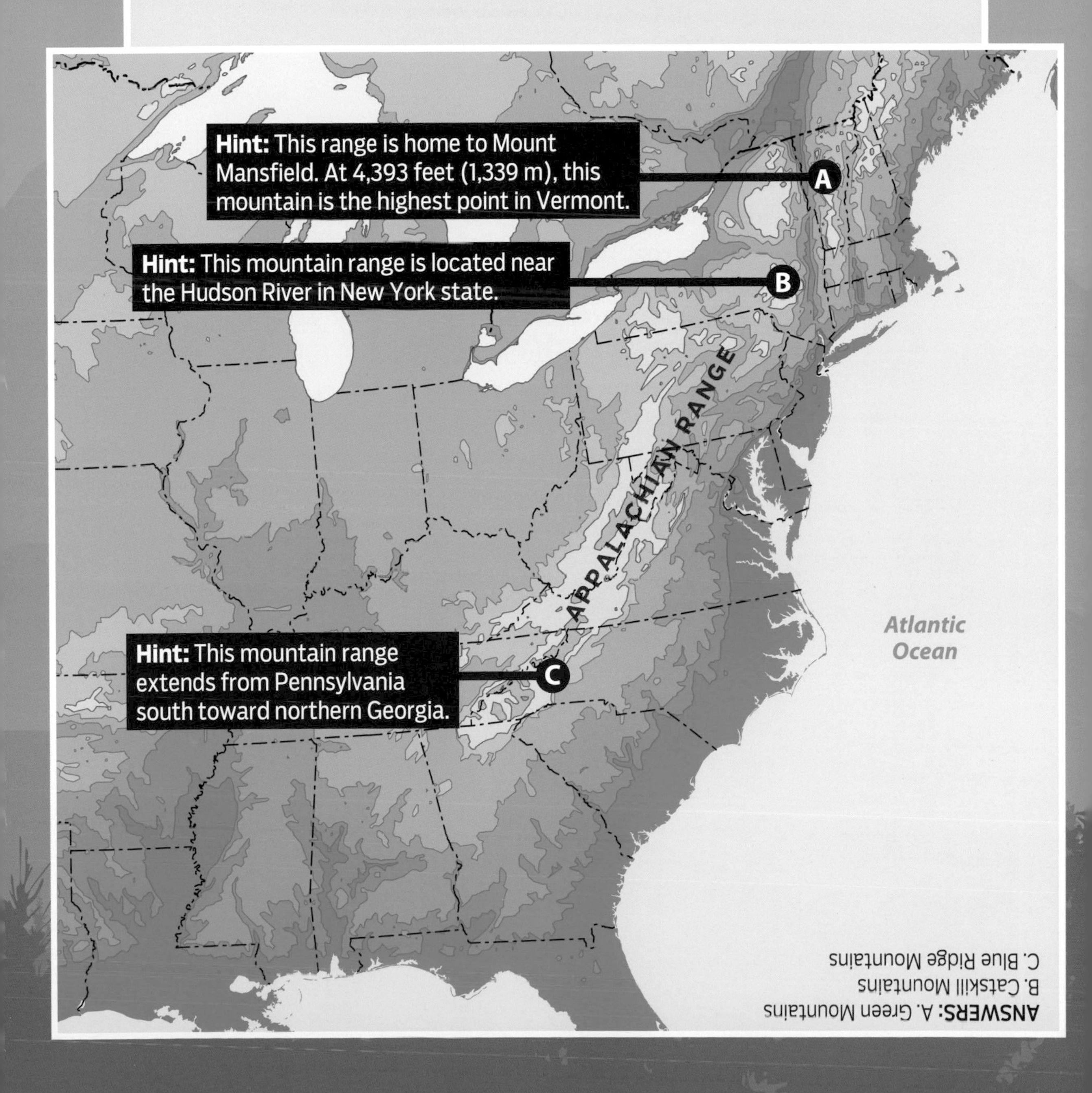

The Rise of the Appalachians

During its early history, Earth was a hotbed of **seismic** activity. As its **tectonic plates** collided, an enormous amount of pressure and heat was created. This changed the **sedimentary** rock of what would become the Great Smoky Mountains into **metamorphic** rock.

After periods of **weathering** and **erosion**, the Appalachian mountain chain finally lifted when two plates crashed into each other. The mountains, including the Smokies, rose so high that they were as tall as today's Rockies.

The plates continued to shift. Older rock was pushed on top of younger rock. This caused a new, rugged landscape to appear. Over time, ice, wind, and water slowly eroded the Appalachians. Their jagged peaks became the rounded mounds seen today.

The oldest sedimentary rocks in the Great Smoky Mountains range are between 800 and 545 million years old.

ON SHAKY GROUND

The same forces that formed the Great Smoky Mountains are still at work today. East Tennessee, which includes the Great Smoky Mountains, is one of the most active seismic areas in the eastern United States. However, the nearby states of South Carolina, Arkansas, Missouri, Kentucky, and Illinois are also affected by events happening underground.

When tectonic plates move, they create cracks in Earth's crust. These are known as faults. Some of these faults can be as thin as a human hair. Others, such as the Great Smoky Thrust Fault, extend for miles (km). The Great Smoky Mountains are home to four major fault lines. When they rub together, the ground shakes.

Part of the Great Smoky Thrust Fault can be seen within the park, at Whiteoak Sink. Small earthquakes often shake the region. Between March and May of 2019 alone, the area recorded eight earthquakes.

The Great Smoky Thrust Fault can be seen behind a waterfall in Whiteoak Sink. It appears in photographs as a horizontal line running behind the middle of the falls.

Plants of the Great Smoky Mountains

Like most of the country's national parks, Great Smoky Mountains National Park is known for its scenic landscapes. However, it is the plant life that makes this park one of a kind. Growing within the park are 1,600 types of flowering plants, more than 100 types of trees, and 100 species of shrubs, along with 4,000 other plant species.

The Smokies range in elevation, rainfall, and **geology**. These factors provide growing conditions for a variety of plants, including some that are **endangered**. The spreading avens and the Virginia spiraea are just two of the endangered flowering plants found within the park.

The crested dwarf iris is one of the many wildflowers found in the park. Found at low to mid-elevations, it is easily recognized by the yellow crest within its purple petals.

GREAT SMOKY MOUNTAIN FORESTS

Forests cover 95 percent of the Great Smoky Mountains. These forests can be divided into five main types.

Spruce-Fir Forest This forest grows high on the mountains, starting at elevations of about 4,500 feet (1,372 m). Most of the trees here are coniferous. They include the Fraser fir and the red spruce.

Northern Hardwood Forests Found at elevations between 3,500 and 5,000 feet (1,067 and 1,524 m), these are the highest deciduous forests growing in the eastern United States. Trees in this type of forest include American beech and yellow birch.

Hemlock Forest Hemlock forests are found at elevations up to 4,000 feet (1,219 m). Biologists have identified hemlock trees in the park that are more than 500 years old.

Pine Oak Forests These forests are found at low- and mid-elevations, often growing on exposed ridges. Chestnut oak, red oak, and white pine are just a few of the trees that grow in this type of forest.

Cove Hardwood Forest These forests are found in sheltered valleys called coves. Their location keeps the trees safe from severe weather. Magnolia and dogwood are two of the most common trees in this type of forest.

Animals of the Park

Of all the wilderness areas on the eastern seaboard, Great Smoky Mountains National Park is among the largest. Many animals take refuge in the park. Here, they have room to roam, find food, and raise their young. The park is home to approximately 65 species of mammals, about 240 varieties of birds, and more than 67 native fish species.

One animal found throughout the park is the American black bear. Biologists estimate that about 1,500 black bears live here. This is about two bears per square mile (2.6 square km). The population is large mainly because the park's black bears are protected by law. They cannot be hunted or harmed in any way.

Birds can also be found throughout the park. The great horned owl, the eastern bluebird, and the field sparrow are just a few birds that can be found flying across the sky. Ground level is home to some of the park's more slithery residents. Some people refer to the park as the "Salamander Capital of the World." This is because it is a prime breeding ground for 30 salamander species.

The Queen Crater snail is the largest land snail living within the Great Smoky Mountains. It can be found at elevations as high as 5,400 feet (1,646 m).

BRINGING BACK THE ELK

Elk were once a common animal in the Great Smoky Mountains. Over time, however, their numbers dwindled, mainly due to overhunting and loss of habitat. By the mid-1850s, both North Carolina and Tennessee had lost their elk populations.

National parks are formed, in part, to preserve the land and the animals that live in it. This sometimes means bringing back animals that have disappeared from the area. In 2001, a project began to re-introduce elk to the park. The first year saw 25 elk brought in. Another 27 elk were added the following year. Since then, the herd has grown naturally. It is estimated that about 150 elk now live in the park.

A male elk can weigh almost 1,000 pounds (454 kilograms) and, including antlers, can stand as high as a pickup truck.

The first group of elk to be re-introduced to the park came from western Kentucky. The second group came from Canada.

A Park Is Founded

When settlers first arrived in the area, they found land that could meet all of their needs. There was fresh water to drink and animals to hunt for food. The forests supplied the wood people needed to build their homes. As more settlers arrived, the need for lumber grew. Lumber mills were soon built throughout the Smokies.

By the mid-1920s, more than 300,000 acres (121,406 ha) of timber had been cut. Some people became concerned about how the lumber industry was changing the land. They felt that the beauty of the Smokies was being destroyed. A movement began to protect the land from further harm.

The movement had the support of many influential people, ranging from writers to politicians. Together, they called on the government to preserve the region. In 1926, President Calvin Coolidge signed a bill to allow the creation of a national park in the Smokies. The park was established eight years later.

Calvin Coolidge was the country's thirtieth president. He held the office from 1923 to 1929.

BIOGRAPHY

Anne Davis (1875–1957)

While a number of people campaigned to protect the Great Smoky Mountains, it was Anne Davis who first mentioned the idea of creating a national park in the area. After visiting national parks in the western United States, she felt that it was the best way to preserve the Smokies. Anne and her husband, a local businessman, founded the Great Smoky Mountains Conservation Association. It worked toward making the park a reality.

Today, Davis is known as the "Mother of the Park." When voters elected her to the Tennessee State Legislature in 1925, she supported a bill to buy 78,000 acres (31,565 ha) from a lumber company. That land became the first parcel set aside for the park.

FACTS OF LIFE

Born: December 27, 1875

Hometown: Louisville, Kentucky

Occupation: Activist, politician

Died: October 3, 1957

THE BIG PICTURE

The United Nations Educational Scientific and Cultural Organization, (UNESCO) has established 701 **biosphere** reserves around the world. The reserves are designed to protect important **ecosystems**, while still allowing for the **sustainable** use of their natural resources. Great Smoky Mountains National Park was named a biosphere reserve in 1988.

North America

South America

Atlantic Ocean

Pacific Ocean

Southern Ocean

Great Smoky Mountains National Park
United States

Waza Biosphere Reserve
Cameroon

LEGEND
- Water
- Land
- Antarctica

N

MAP SCALE 0 — 2,000 Miles / 2,000 Km

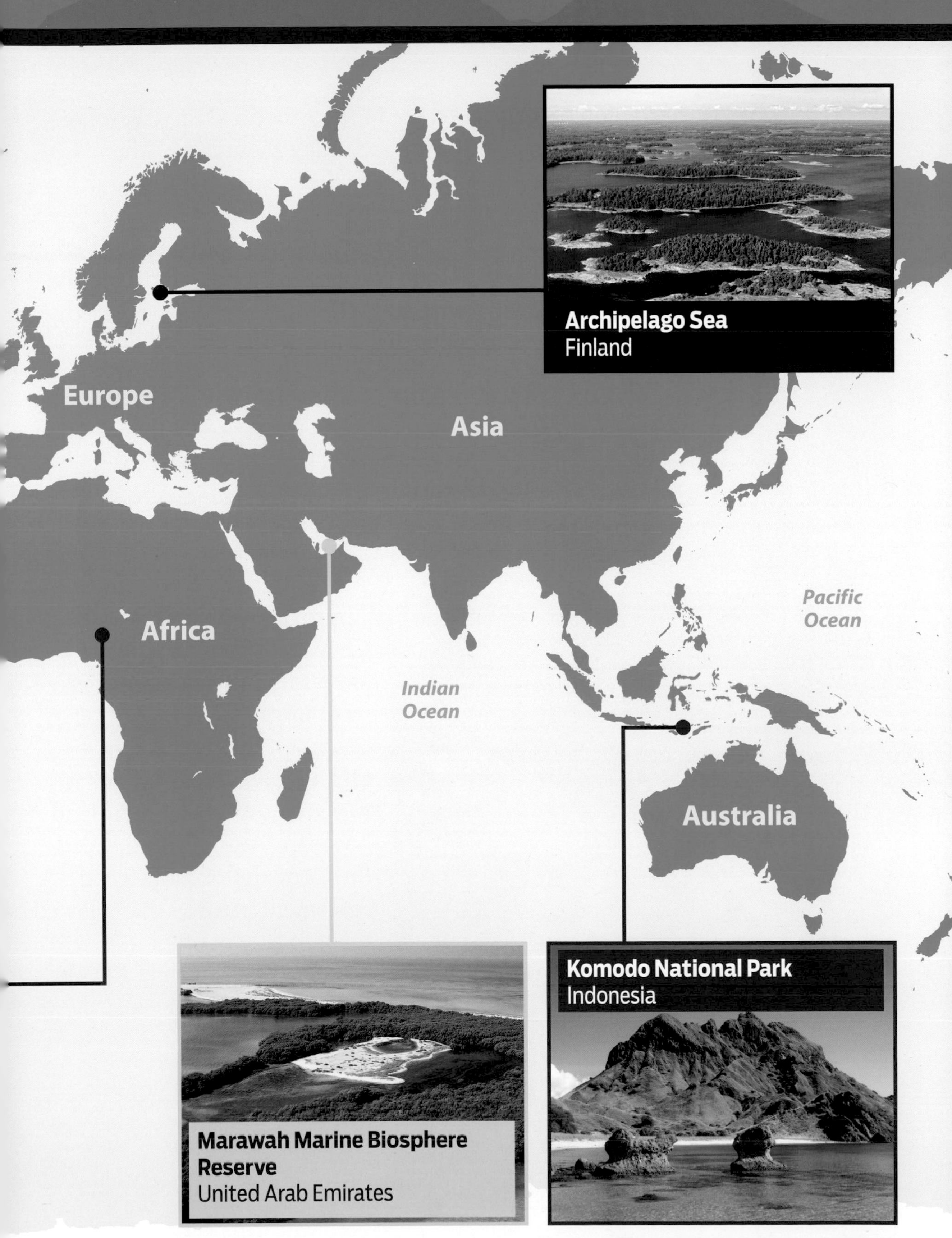
Archipelago Sea
Finland
Europe
Asia
Africa
Pacific
Ocean
Indian
Ocean
Australia
Komodo National Park
Indonesia
Marawah Marine Biosphere
Reserve
United Arab Emirates
Antartica

Home of the Cherokee

Long before Europeans came to the Americas, the Cherokee lived in and around the Great Smoky Mountains. The Cherokee were hunters, traders, and farmers. They lived in small villages along rivers, streams, and in the area's fertile valleys. By the late 1700s, however, the first European settlers had moved to the region, and had begun to clear and farm the land. The Cherokee viewed the settlers as intruders. This led to conflict between the two groups.

Tensions between Native Americans and European settlers took place in other parts of the Southeast as well. In 1830, the government decided to take action. The Indian Removal Act was signed. This allowed the government to remove Native Americans from their ancestral homelands and relocate them elsewhere.

The route taken to Indian Territory is now known as the Trail of Tears. This is because an estimated 15,000 Native Americans died during the journey.

Approximately 100,000 Cherokee, Creek, Seminole, and other Native Americans were forced to move to Indian Territory, in what is now Oklahoma. Not all Cherokee were removed from their land, however. A small band called the Oconaluftee had signed an agreement in 1819 that allowed them to stay in Smokies. Today, approximately 11,000 Cherokee live in the area.

PUZZLER

In the early 1800s, the Cherokee decided to form a government of their own. It was hoped that this would help them work with the U.S. government to reduce the tensions that were developing. The Cherokee government was led by a chief. He was supported by a vice-chief and a council of 32 elected members. Together, they wrote a constitution. This is a document that states a nation's basic laws and principles.

Q. How did the government of the Cherokee Nation compare with the government of the United States?

ANSWER: Both had a person who led the government. In the case of the Cherokee, it was the chief. For the United States, it was the president. Each government had a lawmaking body elected by the people. Each also had a constitution.

TIMELINE

1.1 billion years ago

1550

1650

1750

1.1 billion to 480 million years ago
The rocks that would later make up the Appalachian Mountain chain begin forming.

2.5 million to 11,700 years ago
Continental ice sheets move down from the north, allowing plants and animals from the northeast to **migrate** to the Appalachians.

12,000 years ago
As the climate begins to warm, numerous indigenous groups settle in the area.

1540
Spanish explorer Hernando de Soto is the first European to make contact with the Cherokee in the southern Appalachians.

1795
The Mingus and the Hughes families become the Great Smoky Mountains' first settlers, building homes in the Oconaluftee River Valley.

1889
Qualla Boundary, home of the Eastern Cherokee, is founded.

1940
President Franklin Delano Roosevelt officially dedicates Great Smoky Mountains National Park.

1850

1950

2000

2050

1926
President Coolidge signs the bill to establish Great Smoky Mountains National Park.

1830
President Andrew Jackson signs the Indian Removal Act, and the U.S. government begins relocating the Cherokee and other Native Americans.

2018
More than 11.4 million people visit the park, setting a new attendance record.

KEY ISSUE

INVASIVE SPECIES

Great Smoky Mountains National Park is known for its **biodiversity**. However, recent years have seen the park's native species under threat. **Invasive** species are competing with native species for food and space. This is gradually impacting the park's ecosystem.

One of the plants most affected by invasive species is the hemlock. These native trees are important to the overall health of the park. By providing shade from the Sun, they help regulate the park's air and water temperatures. This creates a livable habitat for birds, insects, fish, and other wildlife.

The hemlock woolly adelgid lays its eggs near the base of a tree's needles. The egg sacs look like small cotton puffs.

Should efforts be made to remove invasive species from national parks?

Yes	No
Invasive species can destroy ecosystems. When they are removed from an area, native plants and animals have room to grow and live. This improves the area's biodiversity.	While some invasive species are destructive, most are not. In fact, some invasive species can bring improvements to an existing ecosystem by providing food for native species.
Some invasive species are linked to the spread of diseases that can be harmful to people.	The herbicides and insecticides used to kill invasive species can damage the environment and people more than the species do.
Invasive species can impact the livelihoods of people who rely on native species for food and income.	Removing invasive species is costly and time-consuming. The money could be spent on more important issues.

However, a tiny non-native insect is slowly killing the park's hemlock trees. The hemlock woolly adelgid was brought to the United States from Asia in the early 1920s. It arrived in the Smokies in the early 2000s. These insects attach themselves to the base of a hemlock's needles and feed on the tree's sap. This deprives the trees of nutrients they need to survive. The needles change color and soon fall off, causing the tree to die.

The park is also being impacted by invasive animal species. Wild hogs were first brought to the area by European settlers, who wanted to hunt them for food. The hog population has grown over time, and there are now hundreds of wild hogs in the park. The hogs dine on the native red-cheeked salamander and destroy wildflower beds. In an effort to reduce their numbers, the park allows the wild hogs to be hunted. Since the 1940s, more than 13,200 wild hogs have been killed or removed from the park.

Park Attractions

Great Smoky Mountains National Park has much to offer those who visit. One of the park's most popular destinations is Clingmans Dome. Visitors can drive up a scenic road from Newfound Gap and walk the remaining 0.5 miles (0.8 km) to the summit. At the top is an observation tower that looks like a flying saucer.

Many people like to visit the park in the fall. This is when the lush, green forests turn into brilliant hues of yellow, red, and orange. Spring is also a colorful time in the park. From late March to early April, the park's wildflowers come into bloom. While some people view the colors from the road, others enjoy seeing them up close by hiking along the park's many trails.

The spaceship shape of the Clingmans Dome observation tower allows visitors to get a 360-degree view of the area.

People have lived and worked in the Smokies for centuries. The park is home to approximately 90 historic buildings from the area's early days of settlement. Visitors can tour historic churches, mills, barns, and cabins dating back to the early 1800s. The village of Oconaluftee is home to the Mountain Farm Museum. Visitors to this museum can learn how early settlers farmed the land. The museum features a farmhouse, barn, chicken coop, and vegetable garden.

CAMPING IN THE SMOKIES

Camping is a popular way to enjoy Great Smoky Mountains National Park. Some people bring their trailers and stay in one of the park's many campgrounds. Others prefer to rough it with a tent in the back country. When doing either, it is important to follow the park's rules. This will ensure the safety of campers, animals, and the environment.

Wildlife Whether a camper or a day visitor, no one is allowed to approach wildlife within 50 yards (46 m). Feeding the park's wildlife is also prohibited.

Pets Dogs and other pets are allowed in campgrounds, but they must be kept inside or on a leash at all times. They can only be taken on two trails within the entire park, but must be leashed there as well. Pets are not allowed in the backcountry.

Food Storage To avoid attracting bears to the campgrounds, food must be kept in a vehicle or camping storage container until it is needed. In the backcountry, food is to be placed on one of the park's bear cable systems. These ensure that the food is kept out of a bear's reach.

Plants Visitors are welcome to view the park's abundant plant life, but all plants are to remain in their natural state. Flowers cannot be picked. Words and symbols cannot be carved into trees.

Cultural Heritage

The Cherokee once made their homes throughout the Great Smoky Mountains. Today, most Cherokee live in Qualla Boundary, which is found on the southern border of the park. It is a place where the Cherokee can maintain their culture and their connection to the land. **Elders** teach traditional crafts, such as basket weaving and mask carving, to younger generations. They also pass on legends from long ago.

The Cherokee enjoy sharing their culture with others as well and offer a variety of programs for visitors. The Oconaluftee Indian Village is one of Qualla Boundary's most popular tourist spots. Here, visitors can see how the Cherokee lived in the past. They can walk inside Cherokee homes, watch a canoe being made, and learn how to shoot a blowgun.

Elders are important to the Cherokee community. They provide support to younger generations and work to preserve Cherokee culture and traditions.

THE HIDDEN LAKE

One of the Cherokee's best-known legends tells the story of a magical lake hidden deep in the Smokies. Called Atagâ'hï, it is an oasis in which birds, fish, reptiles, and other wildlife thrive.

No human had ever seen the lake until a young Cherokee man came to the area. He was seeking quiet and a place to pray. The lake sensed that the man was pure in heart and revealed itself to him. The man was mesmerized by the lake and all of the animals that lived there. After promising never to hunt in the area, he placed a small stone marker at the site and left.

Winter came, and there was little food to eat. The young man and his people were starving to death. To save his people, the man returned to the lake. He shot a bear with an arrow, hoping it would help his people survive the winter. The bear fell into the lake and emerged unharmed. It told the man he had violated the lake and the creatures who lived there. From that time on, the lake was forever hidden from human view.

Fontana Lake is the only known lake in Great Smoky Mountains National Park. With 240 miles (386 km) of shoreline, it is a popular place to kayak, canoe, fish, and paddleboard.

WHAT HAVE YOU LEARNED?

TRUE OR FALSE?

Decide whether the following statements are true or false. If the statement is false, make it true.

1

The Great Smoky Mountains were named for all the wildfires that take place there.

2

Some 15,000 Native Americans died on the Trail of Tears.

3

Forests cover 95 percent of the Great Smoky Mountains.

4

Hernando de Soto was the first European to come in contact with the Cherokee.

5

Ten types of forest are found within Great Smoky Mountains National Park.

6

Invasive species are native to the area in which they are found.

ANSWERS

1. False. They get their name from the natural fog that sometimes covers their peaks.
2. True.
3. True.
4. True.
5. False. The park has five types of forest.
6. False. Invasive species are not native to the area in which they are found.

SHORT ANSWER

Answer the following questions using information from the book.

1 When was the Indian Removal Act signed?

2 What is the name of the park's highest mountain?

3 Who first mentioned the idea of making the Great Smoky Mountain area a national park?

4 How many types of trees are in the park?

5 Which animal was reintroduced to the park in the early 2000s?

ANSWERS
1. 1830
2. Clingmans Dome
3. Anne Davis
4. More than 100
5. Elk

MULTIPLE CHOICE

Choose the best answer for the following questions.

1 How many types of flowering plants are there in the park?

a. 100
b. 1,600
c. 3,000

2 Which U.S. president signed a bill to establish a national park in the Great Smoky Mountains?

a. Theodore Roosevelt
b. Calvin Coolidge
c. Franklin Delano Roosevelt

3 In what year was the park named a biosphere reserve?

a. 1988
b. 1999
c. 2018

4 Approximately how many historic buildings are found within the park?

a. 90
b. 110
c. 135

ANSWERS
1. b 2. b 3. a 4. a

ACTIVITY

CREATE A BIOSPHERE

A biosphere can be as big as Earth or as small as a pond. You can create your own biosphere in a jar with this activity.

Materials

1 large glass mason jar with a lid

2 or 3 hornwort stalks

Water

Potting soil

2 water snails

3 or 4 duckweed leaves

Instructions

1. Place about 1 inch (2.5 centimeters) of potting soil in the bottom of the mason jar.
2. Pour water into the jar until it is about two-thirds full.
3. Place the hornwort stalks in the soil and the duckweed leaves on top of the water. Let the plants and soil settle overnight.
4. The next day, place the snails inside the jar.
5. Put the lid back onto the jar. Place the jar in a warm, bright spot.
6. Keep a record of what happens in the jar each day. Do you see anything growing? Does anything new appear?

Note: You can keep your biosphere for as long as it stays healthy. If you decide to take it apart, your snails should be placed in an aquarium.

KEY WORDS

ancestral: belonging to relatives from the past

biodiversity: the variety of life in a specific place

biosphere: the parts of Earth's crust, waters, and atmosphere that support life

ecosystems: communities of organisms living in the same places

elders: older people who hold respected positions in society

endangered: at risk of no longer living on Earth

erosion: the slow wearing away of something

geology: the study of Earth's physical features and history

invasive: something that intrudes or spreads itself in a harmful manner

metamorphic: rocks that have changed because of heat, pressure, or other natural occurrences

migrate: to move from one place to another

sedimentary: rocks that are compacted and cemented together

seismic: relating to earthquakes or other vibrations of Earth

species: groups of living things that have common traits

sustainable: able to continue over a period of time

tectonic plates: large pieces of Earth's crust

weathering: the destruction of rock by long-term exposure to air and water

INDEX

Get the best of both worlds.

AV2 bridges the gap between print and digital.

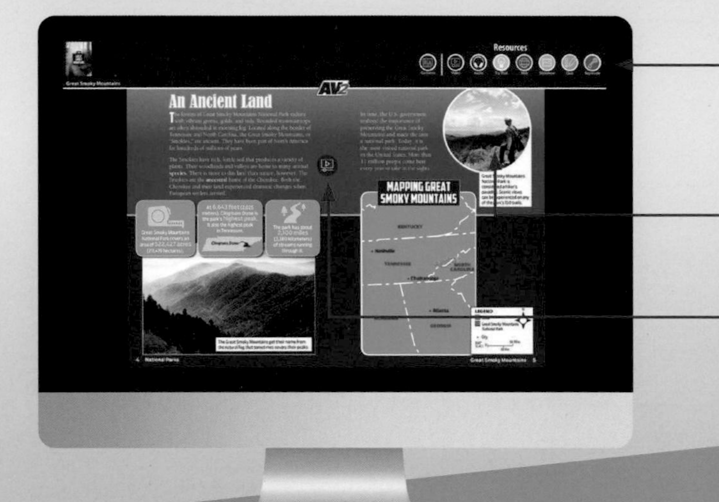

The expandable resources toolbar enables quick access to content including **videos**, **audio**, **activities**, **weblinks**, **slideshows**, **quizzes**, and **key words**.

Animated videos make static images come alive.

Resource icons on each page help readers to further **explore key concepts**.

Published by AV2
350 5th Avenue, 59th Floor
New York, NY 10118
Website: www.av2books.com

Library of Congress Control Number: 2019938451

ISBN: 978-1-7911-1070-3 (hardcover)
ISBN: 978-1-7911-1071-0 (softcover)
ISBN: 978-1-7911-1072-7 (multi-user eBook)
ISBN: 978-1-7911-1073-4 (single-user eBook)

Printed in Guangzhou, China
1 2 3 4 5 6 7 8 9 0 24 23 22 21 20

012020
101319

Project Coordinator Heather Kissock
Designers Tammy West, Ana Maria Vidal, and Terry Paulhus
Captions Heather Kissock

Photo Credits
Every reasonable effort has been made to trace ownership and to obtain permission to reprint copyright material. The publishers would be pleased to have any errors or omissions brought to their attention so that they may be corrected in subsequent printings. AV2 acknowledges Getty Images, Alamy, Newscom, iStock, Shutterstock, and Wikimedia as its primary photo suppliers for this title.